Worrell

Tapping the Sun

A Guide to Solar Water Heating

FIDHEE

WARWICKSHIRE COLLEGE

L I B R A R Y

ROYAL LEAMINGTON SPA & MORETON MORRELL

WARWICK NEW ROAD, LEAMINGTON SPA CV32 5JE

Tel: Leamington Spa 318070

Warwickshire College

00100320

Fifth edition © 2006
The Centre for Alternative Technology Machynlleth, Powys,
SY20 9AZ, Wales
Tel. 01654 705950
Fax. 01654 702782
email: pubs@cat.org.uk
Website: http://www.cat.org.uk
www.ecobooks@cat.org.uk

Written by
Brian Horne (first edition) and revised by Pete Geddes (third edition),
Chris Laughton FIDHEE (fourth edition)

ISBN 1-90217-529-8

Research + Assistance
Sandra Painter & Vicky Reed
Illustrations: Graham Preston
Photographs: Chris Laughton

Printed on 100% recycled paper by
Cambrian Printers 01970 627111

The details in this book are provided in good faith and believed
correct at the time of writing. However, no responsibility is taken for any
errors. Our publications are updated regularly; please let us know of
any amendments or additions which you think may be useful for future
editions.

WARWICKSHIRE COLLEGE
LIBRARY

Class No: 697.78
622-1 LAU

Acc No.
00100320 S

Contents

How to capture a little sunshine

When sunlight falls on a surface, some of the sunlight's energy is absorbed and the surface warms up. Paint the surface matt black and more of the energy is absorbed – the plate gets hotter. Put glazing over the surface and insulation behind it and less of this heat is lost to the air – it gets hotter still. If water flows through pipes attached to a metal surface, then that water will get hot, in fact very hot!

If the surface is a flat metal plate, this constitutes a basic solar water heating collector. The hot water produced by it can be used to heat domestic hot water system in your house.

This simple method can also be used for heating swimming pools or other low-temperature loads. It's not yet really effective at replacing radiators nor can it produce all the hot water we need in winter, however it is still one of the most significant changes a household can make towards reducing global warming and preserving fossil fuel resources.

But it always rains here...

Solar water heating does not need direct sunshine to be effective. Over 200,000 square metres of solar thermal domestic hot water collectors have been installed in the UK to date, which is about 3 square metres per 1000 inhabitants. In the UK, solar panels cannot provide all the hot water for a household's bathing and washing needs throughout the year, but they can provide about 50% of them. They are normally installed in conjunction with a conventional heating system as back-up, and

Solar collectors can be fitted on flat roofs as with this large domestic system.

their performance should be considered in terms of how much fuel, or carbon dioxide emissions, they save.

An average system, used by a 'typical solar owning' household, will provide between 40% and 60% of the fuel used for generating domestic hot water (DHW). This is equivalent to over 1000 kilowatt hours (kWh) per year. A kilowatt hour is the unit of energy normally used to measure electricity or mains gas, and costs about 9 pence at UK standard rate for mains electricity and bottled gas and considerably less for most other fuels.

Solar space heating

In the UK, active solar space heating (heating the air in rooms) is currently limited to a few experimental sites, but in nearby European countries, e.g. Sweden and Denmark, the combination of both solar space and DHW heating is very popular. One of the reasons for this is that they have much better insulated homes than in the UK, so if you have a well-insulated home you might consider solar space heating as well as solar hot water...but you'll still need a back-up heat source.

More commonly, passive solar gain is used where a building is deliberately designed to harness solar radiation through glazing for heating and lighting purposes. This can be achieved through careful sizing and positioning of windows. This important subject is beyond the scope of this book, however, and is well detailed elsewhere.

How much will a solar water heating system cost?

When we ask how much it costs, it's important to understand what is being offered. Some companies may make extravagant claims and some don't make it clear what equipment they intend to supply. After 'shopping around', customers will find that most companies will charge a weighted average of £2,000 to £5,000 for a solar water heating system. Every home is different because we are all different and use varying amounts of domestic hot water in different appliances.

Here are two examples:

John and Sally have just bought a 2-up-2 down terraced house in a town in South Wales. It's got a new roof and the rear faces almost due south with access for a vehicle to the back. They have a washing machine, kitchen and one bathroom, which will soon be converted to a shower room, to create more space, and the existing gas heating is being replaced anyway as it is thirty years old. They just have enough on the mortgage to treat themselves to solar water heating and they want a cost-effective option. They both work long hours and are away at lot at weekends and have no plans for a family. There is firm level ground both front and back of the house and it is in a low limescale area. They contacted some local heating firms and eventually found a few who gave them quotes for solar water and central heating. They were not in a rush and were flexible about when the work was done. They settled for a modest, simple, flat plate 2.5 sq. metre drain-back collector sitting above the roof tiles and an open vented twin-coil copper hot water cylinder of 170 litres total capacity. There was a simple temperature readout of the panel and hot water cylinder as well as a pump operation indicator. The work took two days and in the end they paid £2300 including VAT and two years on-site warranty against faulty parts. They are very happy; their system gives sufficient solar heat that they hardly need their gas boiler in the summer

Peter and Judith live in central London in a large 5 bedroom Georgian three-storey terraced house. They have two teenage children and Peter is retired. The roof is a very old, lead covered flat roof, in a conservation area, and only the south-west is unshaded with no easy parking nearby, a conservatory to the rear and a busy public street to the front. They have two kitchens, a new gas combi boiler, two washing machines and three bathrooms, all with baths and showers, and the interiors are recently decorated. They don't expect to move from their home for a long time and also want fully tested equipment with a high solar fraction*. The combi *boiler is not working well with all the showers and long pipe runs and London is a high limescale area. They want the work done soon before they go on holiday and they contact an experienced solar heating engineer specialist who did a good job for friends of theirs. Ultimately, they settle for 5 square metres of evacuated tube collectors, fixed horizontally on the lead roof and the installer was able to adjust the tubes to improve the angle of pitch. The combi boiler was converted to directly heat the radiators only and indirectly heat a new 400 litre thermal store. An external plate exchanger was fitted in the basement to reduce limescale and allow a high flow rate for the showers. The solar control system included a full diagnostic error display and an energy logging display with computer connection to the rest of the house. The work took five days and they paid £5500 including VAT and a five year on-site warranty against faulty parts and performance. They are very happy with their system and improvements to the shower flow rate, and they have calculated that the system gives them over 60% annual solar fraction. (*See page 17.)*

Will it pay for itself?

As an example, consider a professionally fitted system costing £3000 and expecting to save 1200 units of electricity at 9 pence per unit, giving a simple annual return of £108 on the capital. Not a particularly good return compared with other energy saving measures, but it does compare favourably with keeping the money in a building society. For example; £3000 invested at 3% gross annual interest would return £90 per year. The system could be expected to last 25 years and if fitted well, may not require maintenance expense. Hence the simple total payback is £2700, so in this case full payback is not achieved. Although a gas or oil system may seem to have an even longer payback because of their cheaper delivered fuel costs, it is important to remember that in summer, boilers work very inefficiently whereas solar is performing at its best.

What the above economic analysis shows is that in purely economic terms solar water heating systems are not always a wonderful investment. What we believe at CAT, however, is that there are much worse spending decisions that can be made and that there is a pride and pleasure in heating hot water without pollution year after year. If solar systems were to be fitted in new homes, for example, the costs would be much lower, as they would if fossil fuel prices become higher. If you want to help reduce pollution, fit solar water heating!

Can I do-it-myself?

Installing solar water normally involves working at heights, on a roof, with specialised tools and heavy equipment. None of these tasks should be taken on lightly nor without experienced help and advice. The economics should also be examined – in the UK you will pay a VAT rate of 17.5% for DIY materials but a rate of only 5% if a VAT registered professional does the installation. In addition, there are several grant schemes for solar which exclude DIY installation. Any DIY installation involving replacement of a hot water storage tank also now requires adherence to Building Regulations Approved Document L. If these financial and other physical obstacles don't put you off DIY, you should consider the following options:

- CAT publishes *Solar Water Heating - A DIY Guide*, which includes plans for two types of solar collector and a pump controller, and provides advice on installation. CAT also runs courses on building and installing solar systems.
- 'Solar Clubs' aim to reduce the installation costs of a solar system thus making it a better investment. These clubs are constantly changing so contact CAT for the latest details.

Where can I find a professional installer to do it?

CAT's Solar Water Heating Resource Guide details most of the companies specialising in solar water heating systems in the UK. There is also Solar Trade Association (STA) whose members subscribe to a code of ethical conduct and the Department of Trade and Industry (DTI) keeps a list of installers and suppliers registered by the various current grant schemes. Increasingly, you will see solar collectors installed on other people's roofs and you may be able to get a recommendation from an existing owner. Specialist qualified heating engineers and consultants can also be found through the Institute of Domestic and Environment Heating Engineers (IDHE). Internet search engines can also help track down useful sites, although many engineers are too busy to promote themselves very well! Yellow Pages has a section for solar. Some companies work nationally, with many sub-contractors, and some are small local firms. A considerate installer will always try to personally visit you before giving a quote, carefully checking the condition of your roof, existing hot water system and roof access. They will give you references on request and never pressure you to sign a contract with 'small print' on the night.

How do I choose what kind of equipment to use?

There are over thirty solar collector brands in the UK, many of which are imported.

There are over fifteen UK manufacturers of hot water cylinders and numerous specialised suppliers for pump controllers, as well as multiple choices of sundry plumbing components. At first this choice is bewildering, which is why one of the best ways to make this simple is to find an installer you trust. Above all, an experienced professional should guide you to the appropriate specification for your situation. However, for those of you who want to know more, read on...

Major component groups

There are three main elements within solar water heating systems:

- The Solar Collector
- Heat Transfer System
- Hot Water Storage

The solar collector

What size solar collector do I need?

Not surprisingly, the more hot water you use, the more collectors could be usefully installed, which in turn gives a greater solar fraction (see page 17), but the savings benefits become less dramatic with each successive panel collector added. Manufacturers make collectors in certain fixed sizes to keep them economic to stock, so complicated calculations can become redundant – you may find you have to compromise because of the sizes of available commercial collectors.

As a rough guide, a typical four person household wanting solar DHW requires:

$3m^2$ to $5m^2$ net solar collector area.

This is dependant on collector efficiency, collector orientation, geographical location and the amount of hot water the household uses.

Where should the collectors go on the house?

The optimum pitch angle is approximately the same as most pitched roofs i.e. between 20° and 50° and the orientation between SE and SW. However, by compensating with more collector area, anywhere between east and west or between vertical or horizontal is possible. Try to avoid significant shading of more than 2 hours per spring or autumn day.

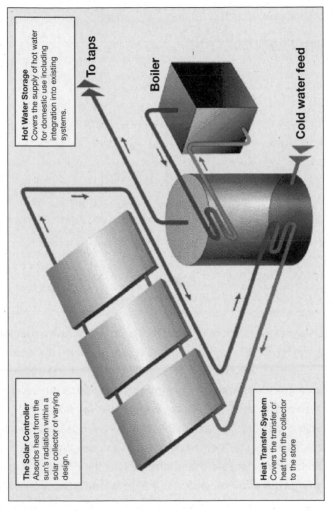

The Solar Controller
Absorbs heat from the sun's radiation within a solar collector of varying design.

Hot Water Storage
Covers the supply of hot water for domestic use including integration into existing systems.

To taps

Boiler

Cold water feed

Heat Transfer System
Covers the transfer of heat from the collector to the store

Fig. 1: System elements for a typical solar water heating installation (c/o SHINE 21, Filsol Ltd.)

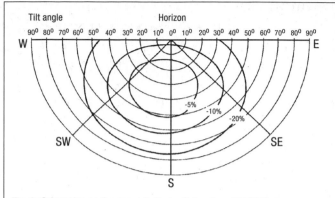

Fig. 2: Orientation performance indicator (taken from BS5918)

Figure demonstrates that if the roof pitch is between 20° and 50°, as is the case for most roofs in the UK, and faces somewhere between east and west, then a solar collector will receive within 20% of the optimum position. With excessively steep or low angles, closeness to south becomes more critical. If desired, collectors can be oversized in less favourable locations or if some shading is present. On ground-mounted frames, the angle can be chosen more accurately, and there are even automatic tracker mounts, which follow the sun each day, which potentially generate even more.

Solar water heating is as dependent on diffuse radiation through the clouds as it is on direct sunlight and so solar collectors do not need to be perfectly south facing or at the optimum pitch angle to work well. In fact collectors can face due west or east and lose only 20% of their output (see Figure 2).

Different collectors are suited to different positions. Some tube collectors can be mounted flat even though the internal absorbers are installed and rotated to face the optimum angle. Some flat plate collectors can be built into roofs to appear flush, like skylights, or onto balcony balustrades and many collectors can be fitted onto a moving tracker device to automatically follow the sun.

The tube collector

The tube collector is usually more advanced in design and manufacture and hence is frequently more expensive. The glass tubes are mounted in rows and individually plugged into a manifold through which the transfer fluid flows. Inside each tube there is often a length of metal absorber that transfers heat to the manifold but sometimes it is just an open flask. Most tube collectors are partially evacuated to reduce convected heat losses that increase the efficiency of the net absorber area. Some use a special 'heat pipe' containing an alcohol that rapidly evaporates to give over-heating protection. Tube collectors cannot normally be integrated into the roof nor used in thermosiphoning or drain back primary systems.

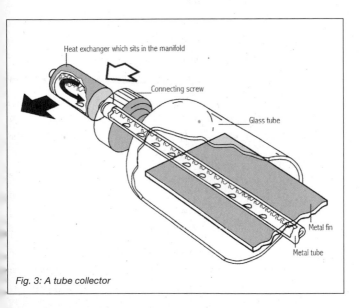

Heat exchanger which sits in the manifold

Connecting screw

Glass tube

Metal fin

Metal tube

Fig. 3: A tube collector

The flat plate collector

The flat plate collector tends to consist of a large sheet of metal containing pockets or pipes holding the transfer fluid. The absorber is held within an insulated box and is generally simpler and cheaper to manufacture than tubes. The glazing may be glass or plastic and this format can be roof-integrated as well as located above the roof. They can also be made partially evacuated and used in thermosiphoning and drain back systems. Flat plates with plastic glazing can be made to custom shapes and sizes. There are also flat plate collectors that use air, instead of liquid, to transfer heat directly into the rooms in the house.

Special collectors for swimming pool systems use absorbers of plastic without glazing or insulation: this is possible due to the lower operating temperatures required in comparison to DHW. Due to the chemical cleaning agent used in pools, metal-based primary components require an indirect system using a heat exchanger.

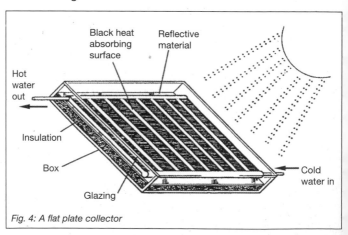

Fig. 4: A flat plate collector

Most modern commercial DHW collectors use selective coatings on the metal absorber behind the glazing to reduce re-radiated heat at high temperatures. Where no heat is extracted from a collector the highest temperature it achieves is called its stagnation temperature and this can vary from 130°C to over 200°C. In operation, the collector operates most efficiently at much lower temperatures, typically 40° to 80°C.

How is the solar efficiency worked out?

The word 'efficiency' when used with reference to solar water heating is often confusing and sometimes quite meaningless. For example, systems are sometimes heavily sold on a so-called 'collector efficiency' factor. The figure they are most likely to be quoting is the optical efficiency of the collector but in fact the response of the collector constantly varies in any real situation because its value depends on the temperature of the ambient air, the temperature of the collector fluids, the insulation of the collector and the angle of the direct sun. Fortunately all these complicated factors can be measured according to a

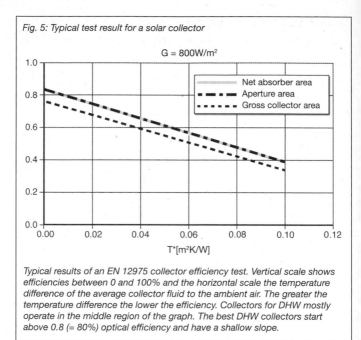

Fig. 5: Typical test result for a solar collector

G = 800W/m²

Legend:
— Net absorber area
— · — Aperture area
— · · — Gross collector area

T*[m²K/W]

Typical results of an EN 12975 collector efficiency test. Vertical scale shows efficiencies between 0 and 100% and the horizontal scale the temperature difference of the average collector fluid to the ambient air. The greater the temperature difference the lower the efficiency. Collectors for DHW mostly operate in the middle region of the graph. The best DHW collectors start above 0.8 (= 80%) optical efficiency and have a shallow slope.

standard European test and the results compared. However the results of this test are not a single, simple figure but instead a series of results such as the graph illustrated (Fig. 5) showing typical results from a test.

Only when a full set of independently tested data is available for each collector being judged can an accurate comparison be made. UK Government funded studies have shown that the collector optical efficiencies and corresponding system efficiencies made little difference to the total annual energy yield, providing the collector area of the lower efficiency collectors were oversized. In the UK to obtain the same yield with common commercial evacuated tube collectors, then the flat plate collector types should be oversized by at least 20% when comparing net absorber areas.

It should be noted that sometimes an unglazed collector appears to have an excellent optical efficiency. This is because it has no glass! Examining the efficiency at higher temperatures and the heat-loss (insulation value) it becomes obvious why these collectors are not suitable for heating domestic hot water, i.e. because as they get hotter, e.g. at DHW temperatures, they also become highly inefficient.

Care should be taken when suppliers mention areas of collectors, as there are at least three ways to use this term and comparisons should use the same one throughout:

Gross area	Largest overall dimension
Net absorber area	All areas that can be heated through the aperture but may be shaded at some incident angles
Aperture area	Unshaded opening that lets light in (or reflects it)

What is the solar fraction?

Given that a solar water heating system is essentially attempting to provide the heat for your domestic washing and bathing water, it is useful to know what percentage of the annual DHW energy it is giving you. This fraction is known as the solar fraction or solar coverage. If a particular month or day is specified, this figure will be different compared to the annual amount. So, for example, if the annual solar fraction is 50%, the summer solar fraction may well be 90% and the winter perhaps only

10%. It also varies depending on the target hot water temperature. A 60°C DHW target temperature will reduce the annual solar fraction by about 10% compared to 50°C.

As an alternative, it is also possible to compare the utilisation fraction of different systems. This is a value that represents a little more closely the value for money or cost per solar kWh of a system and tends to be inversely proportional to the solar fraction. In other words the law of diminishing returns applies when trying to achieve higher solar fractions with large collector areas. Typical utilisation ratios are 30% to 50% and the higher values are obtained with more modest collector sizes where all of the collected solar energy is used up at a low temperature within a short period. As a rule, most UK domestic solar systems are sold with the intention of providing about a 50% solar fraction at 50°C rather than promising high utilisation fractions.

To make life a little easier, computer simulation programs are available to anticipate all the possible variations. These can quickly compare the various scenarios. A specialised solar heating engineer will be able to calculate the required values, although ultimately there are some basic rules of thumb shown below, which also have to be tempered by the real world limitations of stocked sizes of collectors and stores:

- 30–60 litres daily DHW consumption per person (dependent on household)
- 0.5 to 1.5 square metres of collector per person (dependent on collector efficiency, orientation location, target solar fraction etc.)
- 20-60 litres dedicated pre-heat storage per square metre

of collector (typically dependent on space available and target temperature), this is the extra new storage your installer gives you. Add another 80% for the typical total DHW storage capacity.

For example, three people have an average daily consumption of 50 litres each at 50ºC, ie a total of 150 litres per day, and they have an old 110 litre DHW cylinder. They then decide to have a 4m² solar collector, which is to be matched with 120 litres of new dedicated solar storage. This is specially made within a large twin coil cylinder with a total capacity of 250 litres. The existing hot water heating only heats the top part of this cylinder, but even without solar contribution the hot water demand is still met.

The heat transfer system

Which primary system should I choose ?

The components containing the heat transfer fluid, including the solar collector, pipes and heat exchanger, are generally termed the 'primary system'. This is opposed to the term 'secondary system' which refers to components holding the domestic hot water (DHW). Usually the DHW and primary system fluid are different and separated by a heat exchanger, hence forming an indirect system. This exchanger is normally a coil inside the hot water store but can be external. However, in the case where both the primary and secondary fluids are the same, i.e. without a heat exchanger, then the system is direct and the fluid in the collector is therefore plain water. Sometimes an indirect system can have more than one heat exchanger and use air as the transfer medium instead of liquid.

Circulation

For heat to move from the collector to the store, there must be circulation. In normal operation one pipe will flow hot from the collector and the other pipe return cooler, forming a loop moving heat from one end to the other. Due to the layout of most houses, using a pump offers the best flexibility and response to intermittent weather conditions and can permit simple overheating and frost protection. In rare cases, natural thermosiphon circulation can be used without a pump since warm water naturally becomes more buoyant than cold and the fluid moves upwards in the pipes without assistance. However, for this to work satisfactorily the collector must be below the store and the pipes must continually rise upwards towards the store. This arrangement is quite difficult to achieve in practice hence its rarity. Direct types of thermosiphon systems are seldom seen in the UK due to the risk of freezing of the safety vent, which can not be reliably prevented. In addition, prevention of overheating is difficult with thermosiphoning. Overheating and loss of useful heat are drawbacks of using pumps directly coupled to a photovoltaic module without a temperature pump control.

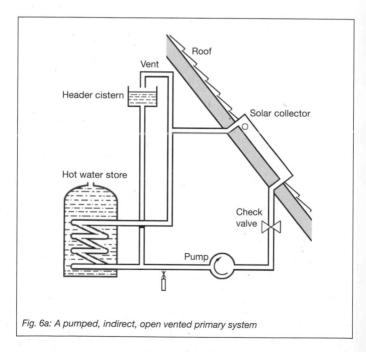

Fig. 6a: A pumped, indirect, open vented primary system

Primary fluid expansion

When water is heated, it will expand (whether stationary or moving) and it is especially important to allow for this in the system design. If there is a fault with circulation under hot/sunny conditions, liquid-based collectors may boil and the contents turn to vapour. There are three main methods of accommodating this safely, one of which must be used somewhere in the primary system:

- A vent to atmosphere into a header cistern (open vent) Fig 6a and 6c
- An expansion vessel and safety valve (sealed system) Fig 6b

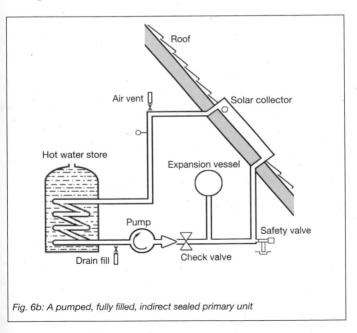

Fig. 6b: A pumped, fully filled, indirect sealed primary unit

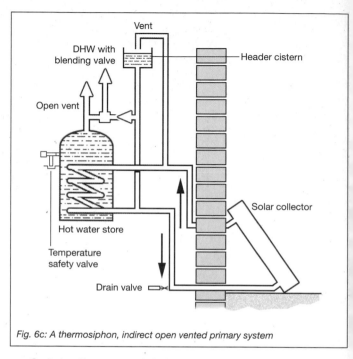

Fig. 6c: A thermosiphon, indirect open vented primary system

• Switch-off pump and drain-away from collector into a vessel (drainback) Fig 6d

Collectors are normally specifically designed for using one of these methods but some can use either.

Protecting from 'freeze' damage

When plain water freezes, it becomes solid and expands causing not only the circulation to cease, but also bursting metal pipes and other rigid elements such as pipes, joints or pumps, which can be dangerous. Some methods to protect against this include:

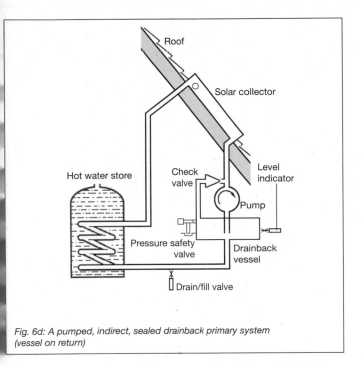

Fig. 6d: A pumped, indirect, sealed drainback primary system
(vessel on return)

- Antifreeze – The most common method found in UK. Uses a special non-toxic, food grade chemical available from plumbing merchants (not car antifreeze). Cannot be used in a direct system. Some old systems use a special oil.
- Drainback – Also common in the UK, where a temperature/light sensor switches the pump off, then permitting the fluid to drain from the collector. Requires careful plumbing to ensure pipes always fall back to a special vessel, which is not always easy to do.

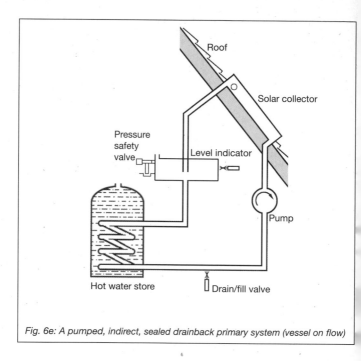

Fig. 6e: A pumped, indirect, sealed drainback primary system (vessel on flow)

- Auto pump control – Triggered by collector temperature sensor. Only recommended if freezing expected a few days a year due to electric pump losses each time it switches on. Can be used with direct systems. A similar principle to electrical trace heating cable fixed onto the water pipes.
- Auto drain down – A valve controlled by a temperature sensitive lever, which opens to dump fluid contents when near freezing. Requires manual refill and only suitable in warmer climates with very occasional freezing.

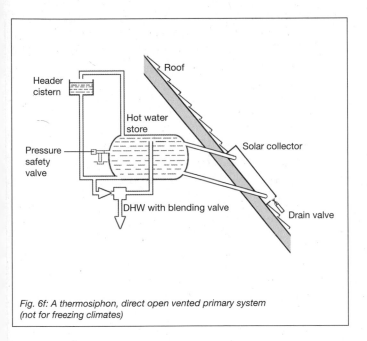

Fig. 6f: A thermosiphon, direct open vented primary system
(not for freezing climates)

- Freeze tolerant – Flexible pipe materials allow freezing without pipe damage, although pump and rigid joints still need protection and any safety vents or devices must continue to work if frozen. Collectors that use air instead of liquid are, in effect, freeze tolerant.
- Insulation – Reduces but never eliminates the chance of freezing.

Controls and measurement

Without any control devices, a solar water heating system can become dangerous due to the difficulty of stopping the sun heating the collector. In an overheating situation, pipes and fluid can become very hot and pressures may rise to the breaking point of the equipment. A well-designed and installed system, which employs the correct control devices, will reduce this risk to an acceptable level. Control devices can also improve system efficiency. A simple thermosiphon system, for example, has almost no control devices on the primary system. Hence it requires extra safety controls on the storage and DHW distribution to limit temperatures.

Measurement devices are sometimes built into controls and permit safe commissioning of the system and provide extra user information. They are sometimes capable of monitoring long-term performance and anticipating operational problems.

A differential thermostat control (DTC) is commonly fitted to pumped systems using sensors fitted into the collector and store. Essentially it compares two sensors for sufficient temperature difference in order that the pump be operated with minimum wasted electricity, but without losing useful collector heat. A typical differential figure would be about 6°C. The DTC will use a lamp to show pump operation and can easily indicate temperatures around the system. A DTC can also switch on a pump to prevent freezing, record historical temperatures (useful for fault finding) and total pump run hours. Advanced DTCs can also vary pump speed to optimise collector efficiency, control auxiliary heating and operate sterilisation cycles to minimize bacteria growth. For a DTC to correctly function, the sensors must be firmly attached to pipe walls and then insulated or, better still, clamped into threaded immersion pockets.

Another form of pump control is a light sensor or small photovoltaic module fixed next to the thermal collector. These still require extra control circuitry to correctly anticipate freezing, stop them pumping-out stored heat or overheating the store. Without this, care should be taken to avoid accidentally returning any usefully stored heat back up to a collector where it will be lost. Photovoltaic modules can also power the pump, which reduces 'parasitic' losses but ideally requires an additional pump control to guard against further losses.

An indication of circulation in all solar primary systems is essential for proper commissioning, ensuring that there is no air in the system and no vapour locks, and setting the correct flow rate for maximum efficiency. A dedicated flow indicator and regulator, featuring a clear glass window and a float, are often used in fully filled systems. An alternative is to use two thermometers on the flow and return pipes, for example on thermosiphoning circuits, although these are only useful if there is solar gain at the time.

Precautions against unwanted reverse heat flow back up from the store are important, otherwise useful heat may be lost. This is because heat already stored will naturally rise back up to the top of the circuit unless restrained. A non-return valve (check valve) fitted in the primary return pipe is common in pumped systems, although a drainback system will inherently provide this function assuming the circulation control is functioning. A DTC also provides this function by comparing the collector to the store temperatures. A thermosiphon system does not have this problem since the collector is positioned lower than the store. Air based collectors must ensure warm air doesn't escape through ceiling vents when the fans are switched off.

Safety in design

Since the sun continues to heat a solar collector even when the demand for heat inside is satisfied, care has to be taken regarding potentially very high temperatures. Sometimes the situation arises undesirably during a circulation failure, i.e. faulty pump or power cut, or deliberately from thermostatic control or storage safety controls. Whatever the reason, there is the potential for over-heating in the primary system, particularly during periods of high summer irradiation where essential over-pressure controls (see above) will be required to safely disperse evaporated liquids. For some older systems, given this scenario, the owner may be required to re-fill the system (re-commission) and ensure normal circulation is correctly returned in the primary system. Older systems used to rely on poorly insulated cylinders or pipework, or even boiling the DHW store, for heat dissipation, however these are acknowledged to be either inefficient, potentially unstable or unsafe.

As an alternative to the above, a modern solar primary system can be designed and installed to automatically and safely resume normal operation by ensuring the following:

- No release to atmosphere of any high temperature fluid (vapour or liquid) under any operating conditions
- Auto-resume of normal operation after stagnation without end-user intervention

A liquid based primary system meeting these criteria can be termed *inherently secure* and this can be achieved with closed (sealed) primary systems containing a vessel capable of holding the entire fluid contents of the collector at all the permitted pressures in the system. Such systems require careful choices of equipment and installation skills but have the advantage that the sun can be 'turned off', unlike earlier system designs, which tended to boil uncontrollably in summer particularly if the storage was undersized.

To be *inherently secure*, all materials in contact with primary system fluids, as well as components such as pipe clips and pipe insulation, should be rated to withstand the full collector stagnation temperature when pressurised, as well as being protected against rodent attack and UV degradation (particularly when external). Many low-cost DIY plumbing materials will quickly fail under these severe conditions and instead specialised components are called for. For new system designs, technical standards exist that can be referred to to ensure safety. Older existing systems may require updating in line with new regulations and standards to ensure optimum safety.

Hot water storage

How do I choose which type of hot water storage?

The hot water that is used by people and appliances, such as in sinks, baths and showers, is called domestic hot water (DHW). The design of DHW stores is a vital part of any solar hot water system as not only do they affect collector efficiency, but they are also the point of interaction with any other heat sources that provide back-up comfort and safety. Unless the solar store is well insulated and has sufficient heat exchanger area (in the case of indirect systems) then precious energy will be needlessly lost. Solar heat does not have to be stored as DHW but in smaller domestic installations usually is.

Incoming cold water can contain chemicals that can become a problem when heated. This is particularly the case in solar systems because they can heat to a wider range of temperatures than conventional heating. Limescale (due to water hardness) can build up a hard crust in kettles and hot water stores and will result in a gradual decrease of the storage, heat exchanger and general solar efficiency. With direct primary systems, the limescale can deposit within the collector itself. Scale reducers are readily available in the UK, although no national standards exist for them and their performance is sporadic. If a house water supply has a high hardness factor ($CaCO_3$ equivalent > 100 mg/ litre) then limescale can be reduced by avoiding heating water beyond 60ºC. One way to do this is by using the solar pump control DTC and/or fitting a DHW store with a cleaning hatch. Using a plate heat exchanger instead of a coil inside the store is

A demonstration solar system at CAT. A cutaway cylinder with integral twin coils can be seen on the right.

even better, because this is much easier to clean and does not 'store' DHW but instead generates it on demand.

There is always a risk of unwanted bacterial growth in all cold and hot water systems. One well-known bacterium is Legionella, which is specifically referred to by UK regulations. A risk assessment of an existing house is best done on site by a suitably informed, instructed and trained person such as an experienced solar engineer. A DIYer should at least inform themselves further on the subject or leave the work to a professional. An inspection requires on-site examination of the cold water supply, secondary storage, distribution and all water appliances. In a domestic scenario, a typical bacteria control measure is to ensure a regular sterilisation temperature within the store. This is easily achieved with a solar store connected to gas, oil or electric, but separate solar pre-heat stores should also engage occasional auxiliary heating (usually by immersion heater).

By law all DWH store temperatures should be controlled to below 100°C (where above 15 litres capacity). With older designs, an extra DHW store or heat-dump radiator may have been used to meet this requirement. Modern solar systems, which use extra safety control devices, permit the use of thermostatic temperature controls without needing such auxiliary components. It is important to confirm which safety controls will be fitted before purchasing any solar system.

Whatever form of DHW heating is used, scalding is a potential risk. The British Burns Association recommends 37° to 37.5°C as a comfortable bathing temperature for children. In some high risk premises the maximum water outlet temperature is set to 43°C. Where DHW might be delivered to showers, baths and taps at potentially scalding temperatures, it is advisable that a method of restricting this is engaged. A suitable device would be a 3-port thermostatic blending valve with a fail-safe mechanism certified to TMV3. As previously mentioned, scale deposition accelerates rapidly above 60°C hence the solar store target temperature should be set in accordance with local water quality. A balance between bacteria safety, scald minimisation and scale reduction requires careful and skilful system design.

Can solar DHW be integrated with my existing household appliances?

A very common problem, confronting solar installers, is the presence of existing DHW appliances such as single-point, multi-point and combi-boilers (oil, gas and electric). These appliances can react unexpectedly to direct solar pre-heating and in some cases this can be dangerous due to potential component failure or scalding. There are some new gas combi-boilers that are claimed to be solar compatible. In all other cases the pre-heating of any of these instant appliances can only be advised with the cooperation of a competent heating engineer. With most existing combi-boilers a modification to one of the stored DHW systems mentioned below should be considered.

Two stores or one?

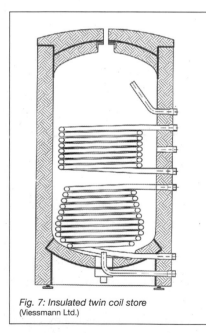

Fig. 7: Insulated twin coil store
(Viessmann Ltd.)

In most UK professional installations, a twin-coil hot water store is used to replace the existing hot water cylinder. Compared to using two separate stores, a twin coil store reduces the surface area of a given volume of water and permits a convenient way to upgrade an existing installation to meet current UK building regulations. A twin-coil store also allows a chance to design in a more rapid and responsive feedback of the solar input to any conventional back-up heat sources, by means of accurate thermostats. A responsive back-up source also allows a more reliable means to sterilise bacteria. Note that because solar heats from the bottom of the store, the warm water then rises to the top where a thermostat connected to the back-up fuel source can respond correctly. This phenomenon creates stratification of the store and ensures the hottest water is nearest the DHW outlet at the top. It also allows fresh cold water to act on the lower solar heat exchanger (usually a coil of pipe) keeping the solar collector return temperature low, to improve efficiency. The downside of twin coil cylinders is that the stores can be too large for some airing cupboards.

An alternative to twin-coil stores is to use two or more separate stores. The solar heat is first transferred to a new dedicated single coil preheat cylinder. When a tap is opened, the solar heat moves to the existing store whereupon extra heat is added for comfort or sterilisation. This can be easier to install alongside existing installations and permits large storage volumes whilst retaining flexibility. However this configuration can 'trap' solar heat in the first store if there is no DHW draw off and hence the final store may be needlessly heated by an automatic boiler or immersion. Note also that each store must have independent expansion and safety devices. If a new pre-heat store is to be added then some form of sterilisation, (i.e. from another heat source) should be installed into the new preheat store for occasional cleansing.

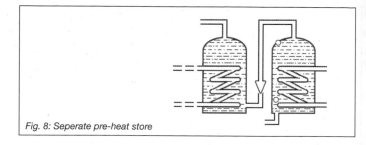

Fig. 8: Seperate pre-heat store

How do I choose a high performance solar store?

Tall narrow cylinders improve solar performance due to increased *stratification* between the cold water at the bottom and the hot water at the top. This means that more solar heated water can be drawn off without cooler, fresh water feeding into the cylinder. Specially manufactured solar cylinders, which have a high level of insulation, can be obtained that also have an extra large coil to facilitate heat exchange. This is located at the bottom of the store, where a baffle is placed also to avoid spoiling the hot water stratification. Sensor pockets are located to accommodate any temperature probes connected to a pump control system.

It is best to size the lower 'solar' part of the store so that it is at least 80% of the average daily hot water usage. This pre-heat volume is not normally heated by any other heat source. So, the total overall volume of the store therefore includes the pre-heat plus the conventional stored volume. For most dwellings with a modern solar collector this is unlikely to be less than 150 litres. Under-sizing of the cylinder can lead to over-heating in summer, limited domestic hot water availability and a low solar collector performance.

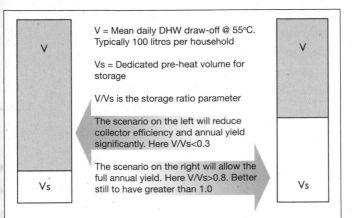

V = Mean daily DHW draw-off @ 55°C. Typically 100 litres per household

Vs = Dedicated pre-heat volume for storage

V/Vs is the storage ratio parameter

The scenario on the left will reduce collector efficiency and annual yield significantly. Here V/Vs<0.3

The scenario on the right will allow the full annual yield. Here V/Vs>0.8. Better still to have greater than 1.0

Fig. 9: The importance of a dedicated pre-heat volume for solar storage

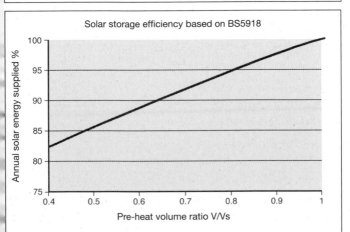

Fig. 10: If dedicated solar storage is undersized, the annual performance will be reduced. To realise the full potential of a solar collector, there needs to be a large enough store for solar heat. This store must not be heated from other heat sources since then it will lack the capacity to take more heat during the day. The amount of energy lost in a year due to inadequate pre-heat storage can be calculated from this graph. A typical household requires at least 80 litres dedicated pre-heat storage.

What general type of DHW store is right for me?

There are several choices of store configuration including vented, unvented or thermal store. This choice is usually taken considering what is already in use and any DHW appliances that may be used in the future. Of key importance is the chosen operating water pressure of the secondary system. This choice may restrict the collectors and primary systems that can be used. The following are a few of the common choices:

Vented

Fig. 11

Typically low pressure i.e. below 1 Bar. Very common in UK and Ireland but not in the rest of the world. Requires a cold-water store (CWS) high enough to give adequate pressure to the highest outlets. The CWS can provide a reserve if the incoming main fails. The CWS is at risk of freezing (in a loft) and contamination (overheating and dust) if poorly installed. Typically an economic choice in the UK with custom vented copper cylinders readily available. May be at risk to limescale inside store but, with an integral hatch, can be cleaned. Stainless steel is possible for maximum durability.

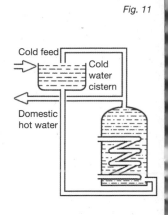

Cold feed

Cold water cistern

Domestic hot water

Unvented

Capable of high pressure (up to 3 Bar) if there is a sufficient incoming cold main supply. Increasingly common in UK. Dangerous if installed incorrectly hence requires a qualified, competent installer in the UK. No 'tanks' in the loft but little reserve when the main fails. Heavier and more expensive to manufacture. May be at risk to limescale inside store but, with a hatch, can be cleaned. Custom choices not so easily available. Copper, steel coated and stainless steel options.

Fig. 12

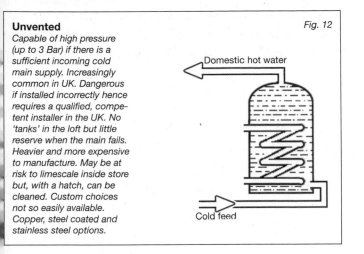

Domestic hot water

Cold feed

Thermal store with integral coil

Capable of high pressure (up to 3 Bar) if there is a sufficient incoming cold main supply. Mixture of high pressure DHW inside a coil surrounded by a low-pressure store. Requires higher temperatures to provide sufficient hot water for large draw-offs hence can be more inefficient. No 'tanks' in the loft but little reserve when the main fails. May be at risk to limescale inside integral coil. Custom choices not so easily available. Copper, coated and stainless steel options.

Fig. 13

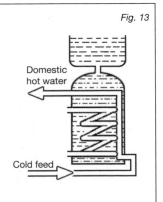

Domestic hot water

Cold feed

Thermal store with external plate exchanger

Fig. 14

Capable of high pressure (up to 3 Bar) if there is a sufficient incoming cold main supply. Mixture of high pressure DHW inside the heat exchanger with a nearby low-pressure store. Requires higher temperatures to provide sufficient DHW on large draw-offs, and a pump and flow-switch, and hence can be more inefficient.

In effect, there is no DHW storage – it is 'instantaneously' gener-ated. External exchanger typically demountable and stainless steel, hence very hygienic and easy to control and clean lime scale. No 'tanks' in the loft, hence little reserve when the main fails.

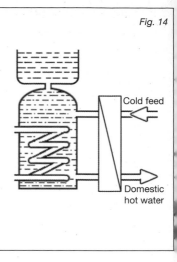

Cold feed

Domestic hot water

Operation and maintenance

A typical solar water heating primary system would benefit from the following annual inspection checks.

- The glazing seals are weather-tight and sound.
- Collector glazing is undamaged.
- Collector glazing is reasonably clean.
- Where visible, absorber paintwork or coating is sound.
- The roof fixings are firm and the roof covering satisfactory by visual inspection.
- The fluid levels in the cistern, drainback vessel or pressure gauge checked against tolerances.
- Electrical controls and temperature sensors are operating correctly.
- The circulating pump, if fitted, is operating without due noise.
- Pipework insulation is firmly in place.
- No condensation or damp spots are apparent, particularly around the pipework and fixings in the roof space.
- All safety and information labels are in place.
- Every five years the antifreeze, if present, should be tested. Some antifreeze products require regular replacement. For direct primary systems, regular de-scaling may be required.

Manufacturer's instructions, where available, are best used in preference. A user should not put themselves in danger in order to carry them out.

If there is a significant drop in pressure or fluid level suspect one or more of the following:

- Overheating may occur during a period of hot weather if the pump isn't operating, and the heat transfer fluid is therefore not being circulated (e.g. during a power cut, holiday, etc.). Thermal energy is not being removed from the collector so the water temperature will rise, hence water volume and system pressure could increase. This could result in the release of hot water or steam from the pressure relief valve or the automatic/manual vent. When the system returns to normal operating conditions the pressure will reduce due to the loss in fluid volume.
- If water is escaping from the system the volume of water in the system decreases and hence the pressure/fluid level will drop. If there is a leak in the system it may require a drain down and repair/replacement of the faulty component.

The main reasons why some older solar water heating systems might malfunction are:

- Frost damage to the collector due to degradation of antifreeze.
- Temperature sensors displaced from the correct position
- Circulating pump seizes.
- Loss of fluid due to open vent evaporation or slow leak, often through automatic air vent.
- Sealed system expansion vessel has lost pre-charge.
- Residue from overheated antifreeze blocking pipes.
- Limescale blocking the collector or heat exchanger.

The main reasons why some solar water heating systems perform poorly are:

- Temperature differential between tank and panel wrongly set within solar controller.
- Pump control missing or malfunctioning.
- Other heat appliance interfering with transfer in DHW store.
- Missing or damaged insulation of pipes and store.
- Incorrect location of temperature sensors.
- Inadequate air removal from pipes.
- Incorrect pump speed.
- Solar storage too small.

Are there any legal issues?

The local planning authority should be approached to check whether town and country planning approval is required for the installation of a solar water heating system. Normally planning consent won't be required, but when the building in question is to be newly built, a listed building or is in a conservation area or an Area of Outstanding National Beauty (AONB) consent may be needed. In such cases, planners will be concerned about issues like appearance and visual impact above the roof line (they apply similar strictures to satellite dishes and skylights). Often, even when there are concerns, they can be alleviated by careful siting of collectors on the roof, or at ground level.

Check with your insurers and mortgage company that they are happy for the modifications to be made.

The following interpretations should not be taken as the full meaning of the law. Any actions intended to be based on the law should refer to copies of published legislation, typically

available from HMSO, or advice sought from a qualified practitioner of law.

All fittings in contact with mains water are covered under the Water Supply (Water Fittings) Regulations 1999. This includes all components or fittings in a secondary system supplied from a utility and all components and fittings on a direct solar system. Responsibility of compliance lies with the householder, DIYer and installer, although certain approved contractors can issue certificates of compliance, which provide immunity from prosecution to the householder. All solar water heating work is therefore notifiable to the water utility and permission must be awaited for ten days (after which, if you haven't heard anything you can go ahead), except when installed in extensions or alterations of water systems in existing houses. No water must be stored in domestic premises above 100°C and avoidance of water contamination and undue consumption is mandatory. There are constraints on temporary connections to the water mains often used in filling a primary system. There are several schemes to become an approved contractor – i.e. WEAPS, IoP ACPS, SNIPEF, APHC, as well as with some individual water companies (Anglia, Severn Trent, Yorks, Thames) – for the installation of solar water heating systems.

The Building Regulations 2001, AD Part L1 apply to all to solar installations, including those by DIYers, particularly those that involve changing a hot water store in a dwelling. Each installation requires certification to be left on site, which only a competent person can signify, confirming that minimum technical and mandatory standards have been met. Unless deemed competent to connect a particular heat appliance (i.e. CORGI for gas, OFTEC for oil or HETAS for solid) or competent for the particular secondary solar store (i.e. HSE G3 for un-vented) then individuals working on the installation, including DIYers, must instead notify the local council's building control department who will issue certification. There are constraints on secondary store designs, thermostats, timers, boiler interlocks and insulation. The terms of competency for some secondary stores are currently under review.

The Pressure Equipment Regulations 1999 require most fluid solar systems to be safe and designed and manufactured according to sound engineering practice. This applies to those who place functional assemblies equipment on sale, but can apply to those who assemble custom systems. For large-scale collectors it can mean 'CE' marking of components and that a third party body is involved.

The Health and Safety Executive (HSE) are responsible for enforcing many construction oriented regulations – mostly applying to paid workers, although some do apply to DIYers as well. These are extensive and not solar specific so are not listed here. The HSE have many excellent books and websites to refer to as well as telephone helplines.

Resources

General organisations

Association of plumbing and heating contractors
14 Ensign House, Ensign Business Centre, Westwood Way,
Coventry, West Midlands CV4 8JA.
Tel. *024 7647 0626*   **Fax.** *024 7647 0942.*
email. *aphcuk@aol.com*
website *www.licensedplumber.co.uk* & *www.aphc.co.uk*
Trade association to the plumbing industry. Its members give a
warranty on work done, to cover any costs arising from faulty
work. Involved in SHINE 21 – training plumbers in solar water
heating.

Centre for Alternative Technology
Llwyngwern Quarry, Pantperthog, Machynlleth, Powys SY20 9AZ.
Tel. *01654 705989*   **Fax.** *01654 702782.*
email. *info@cat.org.uk*   **website** *www.cat.org.uk*
CAT's key areas of work include renewable energy,
environmental building, energy efficiency, alternative sewage/
water treatment and organic growing. Provides a unique
7 acre visitor demonstration centre open 7 days a week,
facilities for schools/colleges, a free information service,
consultancy, public courses, publications, a mail order service,
quarterly 'Clean Slate' magazine and a membership scheme.
Specifically it runs short residential courses on solar water

heating and DIY solar water heating and also supplies clip fins for DIY systems via mail order.

Institute of Domestic Heating and Environmental Engineers

Unit 32C, New Forest Enterprise Centre, Chapel Lane, Totton, Southampton, Hampshire SO40 9LA.
Tel. *02380 66 89 00*   **Fax.** *02380 66 08 88.*
email. *info@idhe.org.uk*   **website** *www.idhe.org.uk*
Independent non-profit making professional body, which aims to promote energy efficient domestic central heating components and the installation of safe and efficient systems, without detriment to the environment. Has information on its website about renewable sources of heat including solar water heating, biodiesel, wood and heat pumps.

Institute of Plumbing and Heating Engineering

64 Station Lane, Hornchurch, Essex RM12 6NB.
Tel. *01708 472791*   **Fax.** *01708 448987.*
email. *info@iphe.org.uk*   **website** *www.iphe.org.uk*
Trade body for plumbing and heating professionals. Members have to prove their competence through recognised qualifications or extensive experience.

My Solar

website *www.mysolar.com*
Website with lots of information on the different types of solar energy and how to make use of them. Includes technical information on solar water heating and solar electric (PV) systems.

Network for Alternative Technology & Technology Assessment (NATTA)

c/o EERU, The Open University,
Milton Keynes, Buckinghamshire MK7 6AA.
Tel. *01908 654638*   **Fax.** *01908 654052.*
email. *S.J.Dougan@open.ac.uk*
website *http://eeru.open.ac.uk*
Membership organisation with bi-monthly newsletter 'Renew',
containing up-to-date information about all aspects of
renewable energy. EERU runs a course on Sustainable Energy
within the Open University's undergraduate programme and
supports a range of post-graduate research work.

Scottish Solar Energy Group

Prof. Colin Porteous, Mackintosh School of Architecture,
167 Renfrew Street, Glasgow G3 6RQ.
Tel. *0141 353 4657*   **Fax.** *0141 353 4740.*
email. *c.porteous@gsa.ac.uk*   **website** *www.sseg.org.uk*
Promotes solar energy in Scotland by running conferences,
seminars, field trips and competitions. Membership of 60,
mostly architects, engineers and students but open to all.

Solar Clubs Project (Bristol)

c/o The Centre for Sustainable Energy, The Create Centre,
B-Bond Warehouse, Smeaton Road, Bristol BS1 6XN.
Tel. *0117 930 4097*   **Fax.** *0117 929 9114.*
email. *mark@cse.org.uk*   **website** *www.cse.org.uk/renewables*
Scheme run across the country. See website to find local
Solar Club. Not-for-profit initiative that organises supplier

discounts through bulk purchases, training and and support to provide DIY solar water heating systems at a much reduced price. Prices expected to be between £1000 and £1500. Runs professional training for those wanting to install solar water heating in their homes.

Solar Trade Association Ltd

The National Energy Centre, Davy Avenue, Knowlhill,
Milton Keynes, Buckinghamshire MK5 8NG.
Tel. *01908 442 290* **Fax.** *0870 052 9194.*
email. *enquiries@solartradeassociation.org.uk*
website *www.solartradeassociation.org.uk*
Aims to maintain standards within the solar water heating industry and to promote the use of solar power in general. Codes of conduct and list of members available. National enquiry centre.

The Solar Energy Society (UK-ISES)

c/o School of Technology, Oxford Brookes University,
Headington Campus, Gipsy Lane, Headington, Oxford OX3 0BP.
Tel. *01865 484 367* **Fax.** *01865 484 263.*
email. *ukises@brookes.ac.uk*
website *www.thesolarline.com*
UK branch of the International Solar Energy Society. Promotes all forms of solar and other renewable energy. Communicates ideas and developments through conferences and publications. Membership open to both professionals and interested lay-people. Can give contacts for other branches worldwide.

Grants

Community Energy Programme (Energy Saving Trust)

Tel. *0870 850 6085.* **Fax.** *none.*
email. *communityenergy@est.co.uk*
website *www.est.org.uk/communityenergy*
Offers funding, information and support to Local Authorities,
Registered Social Landlords, Universities, Hospitals and other
public service organisations for the refurbishment of existing
and installation of new community heating schemes.
£50 million available for capital grants, also development
grants for option appraisal and developing business plans.
The Programme also provides a series of tools and information
for potential applicants. It is jointly managed by the Energy
Saving Trust and the Carbon Trust on behalf of DEFRA.

Energy Saving Trust / Grant Information Database

Tel. *0845 727 7200 / 0800 512 012* **Fax.** *none.*
website *www.est.org.uk/myhome*
Website and helpline with advice on how to save energy in
the home, and how to find your nearest Energy Efficiency
Advice Centre. Provides a single, central source of information
about domestic energy efficiency grants and offers. The 0845
helpline can also give advice to professionals about training in
installation of energy efficient equipment.

Low Carbon Buildings Programme

Tel. *0800 915 7722* **Fax.** *none.*

website *www.lowcarbonbuildings.org.uk*

DTI grant scheme to help with the cost of low carbon microgeneration technologies for householders, community organisations, schools, the public sector and businesses. Administered by the Energy Saving Trust, with support from the Carbon Trust on larger projects. Applicants must have taken certain energy efficiency measures in order to be eligible.

Nie Smart

Woodchester House, 50 Newforge Lane, Belfast BT9 5NW.

Tel. *028 9068 5089* **Fax.** *028 9068 5035.*

email. *online form*

website *www.niesmart.co.uk*

Programme of support for renewable energy and energy efficiency technologies, run by Northern Ireland Electricity. Gives support to householders, communities, businesses, and housing providers. Covers biomass, solar water heating, photovoltaics (PV), ground source heat pumps, micro-combined heat and power (CHP) and small-scale hydro. The support is additional to the Clear Skies and Solar PV Grant schemes.

Scottish Community & Householders Renewables Initiative

Tel. *0800 138 8858* **Fax.** *none.*

email. *online form.*

website *www.est.org.uk/schri*

Scottish Executive funded scheme offering grants, advice and project support to develop and manage new renewables, for both households and communities. Covers small-scale wind power, automated wood fuel heating, solar water heating, small-scale hydro power, and heat pumps (ground, air and water source). Scottish Equivalent of the Clear Skies Scheme.

Solar City
c/o EnergyTech Ltd, 1 High St., Clydach, Swansea SA6 5LG.
Tel. *01792 846 404*   **Fax.** *01792 849 000.*
email. *info@solarcity.co.uk*
website *www.solarcity.co.uk*
EU funded project to help SME's (small & medium sized enterprises) in the South West Wales area install solar water heating systems. It can also help with training for plumbers.

Solar for London
Southwark Energy Agency, 42 Braganza St., London SE17 3RJ.
Tel. *020 7820 3156*   **Fax.** *020 7582 4888.*
email. *info@solarforlondon.org.uk*
website *www.solarforlondon.org*
Householders in certain London boroughs can claim an additional 'Solar Reward' (on top of the £400 Low Carbon Buildings grant) towards the cost of a professionally installed solar water heating system

The Carbon Trust
8th Floor, 3 Clement's Inn, London WC2A 2AZ.
Tel. *0800 085 2005 or 020 7170 7000* **Fax.** *020 7170 7020.*
email. *info@thecarbontrust.co.uk*
website *www.thecarbontrust.org.uk*
Publicly funded body to assist with the transition towards a low carbon economy, specifically working with business and the private sector. Offers advice, free consultation, and funding such as low interest loans for energy efficiency equipment. The Low Carbon Innovation Programme, including the Foundation Programme, funds the development of new and emerging low carbon technologies.

RECEIVED
1 5 NOV 2006